PUBLISH YOUR BOOK USING

CREATESPACE

Yael Eylat–Tanaka

CONTENTS

INTRODUCTION

Self-publishing is all the rage these days. Hopeful authors have sprung up everywhere. Armed with a computer and a head full of lofty ideas, everyone, it seems, is self-publishing novels, poetry, videos, and the like, some whimsical, others more academic and serious. And with all these new capabilities, the more creative and imaginative among them have found ways to expand on the traditional methods of marketing and promoting their services by writing blogs, articles, eNewsletters, and more.

This book addresses a new concept: that of writing a book to serve in lieu of the time-honored business card.

Consider what a book can do, and what you can accomplish by writing a book. A book is a compendium of a great deal of information, including your company or services, your experience, your expertise, testimonials and referrals, your accomplishments, as well as a thorough description of your services, pricing structure, or guarantees. A book that is well written conveys not only a great deal more information than a business card, but also implies greater value and professionalism.

Depending on your subject matter, a book may also be valuable on its own merits, and may in itself produce a significant side income.

Why CreateSpace?

There are several self-publishing concerns on the Internet, some free, some not. Some names in the space include:

- IngramSpark
- Smashwords
- Blurb
- Lulu
- CompletelyNovel

And many more.

They all have plenty of tools, design panels, covers, fonts, and distribution capabilities to disseminate your book to the far reaches of the world. Each platform has its own methodology for creating a book, some more user-friendly than others, but they all accomplish the same thing: publishing books online and in print.

Here we will go over the steps required to publish your book using the CreateSpace model. CreateSpace is well known, has been around for a long time, and is owned by one of the most prolific online marketplaces in the world, a marketplace that, coincidentally, started out selling books.

CreateSpace is the platform owned d by Amazon.com to facilitate self-publishing physical books. With free online tools that include a cover creator and previewer, as well as worldwide distribution capabilities, carrying inventory is no longer necessary. Your book is available on demand through Amazon, Kindle, eStore, or may even be handed out as your business card.

A book as a business card? Yes!

Those little 2 x 3.5-inch business cards of old convey very little information about you or your services, and are all too often discarded. A book, by contrast, can be a source of rich details about everything from your company's vision to a background of your experience and accomplishments. You may describe your services in greater detail, and provide deeper treatises of the complexities that you help resolve.

So let's jump right in and go through the steps necessary to create a book using CreateSpace.

Creating Your Account

Before you can begin manipulating the tools to format your book, you must create an account. In the address field of your browser, type https://www.createspace.com. The window that opens looks like this:

In the top left-hand corner is the log-in section. If you are new to the site, you must sign up in order to create your account. Once you have signed up with your user name and desired password, you may log in. At this point, you will be redirected to your Member Dashboard. Please note that the images shown here are of my own account, and therefore will reflect some details that apply only to me.

The Dashboard

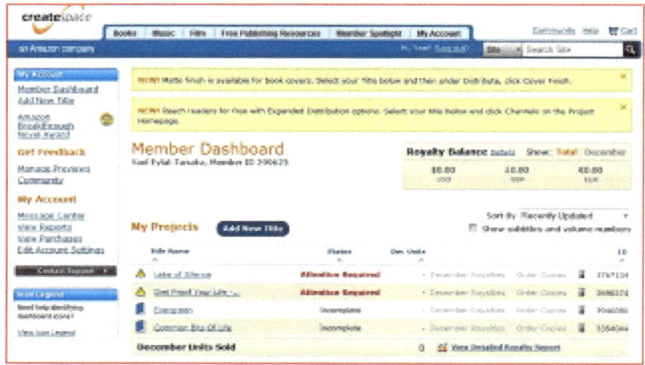

Note that on my dashboard are listed four books, two of which have the notation "Attention Required" in red, and the other two are listed as Incomplete. Above that list is the heading, My Projects, and next to it is a radio button to "Add New Title." This tutorial explains how to use CreateSpace. Once we have clicked on Add New Title, the following screen opens up, leading the way to starting our new project.

If you follow these instructions step by step, and refer to the images included in the tutorial, you are likely to be successful in your new venture. Do not become confused or overwhelmed. I'm here to help.

We have now clicked on Add New Title, and this act will bring us to the next panel, Start Your New Project.

Start Your New Project

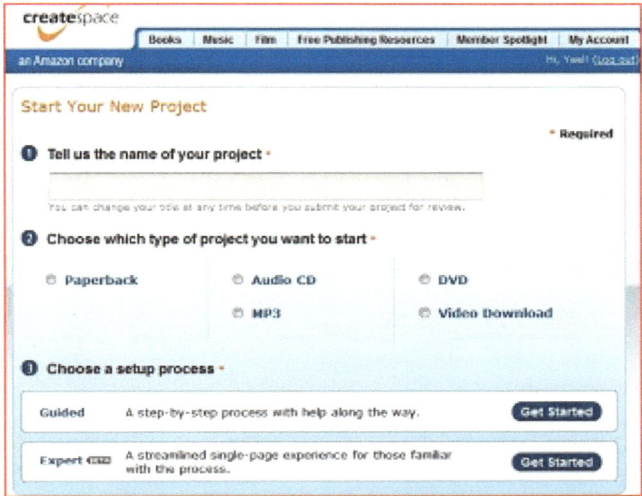

This panel is divided into three major steps. Step 1 is labeled, "Tell us the name of your project." In the space provided, we'll type in the name of our book, *Publish Your Book Using CreateSpace.*

Step 2 on this panel asks us to choose the type of project: Audio, MP3, or other. We'll choose Paperback and click next to it.

Step 3 gives us the option of setting up our book using the Guided application, chock-full of detailed steps, or the so-called Expert application, a more streamlined version for the experts among us. For our purposes, we'll select the Guided option, and click the radio button called Get Started.

We are now redirected to a panel called "Title Information."

Title Information

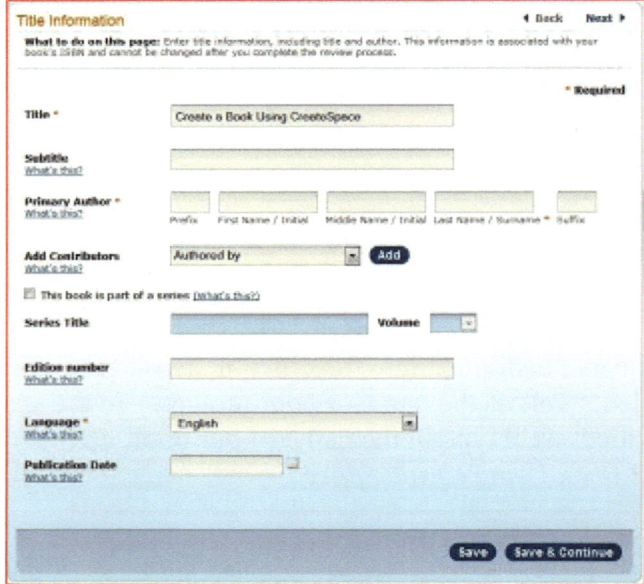

Note that the first item on this panel, Title, is automatically filled in with our previously-selected book title.

The next line asks for a subtitle to our book. Let's embellish our title with a short description, such as *If you absolutely MUST do it yourself!*

The Primary Author line is self-explanatory. I'll enter my own name. Underneath the author's name is a space to add other contributors to your project, and a space to indicate if this book is part of a series. In our case, it is a standalone version, so we will leave this blank, and move right on down to Edition Number, where I will fill in with 1. The next line is filled in with English, and the last line on this panel is the Publication Date. Let's type in December 25, 2013. Don't forget to Save, or better yet, Save & Continue, bottom right radio button.

We are now redirected to the next page, requesting the ISBN number.

The ISBN

An ISBN is a distinct number assigned to every book published. You can select an individual custom ISBN, a universal ISBN number, or the free ISBN number provided by CreateSpace. In keeping with our mission of free, we'll select this option and click on the first available option. That will rearrange the panel a tad to look like this:

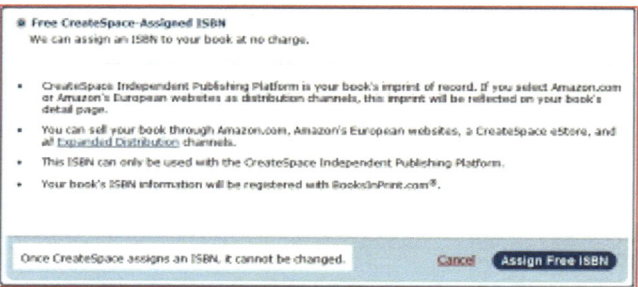

Click the lower right-hand radio button that says Assign Free ISBN. Once your ISBN number has been assigned, you will be redirected to the panel that lists your distinct ISBN number:

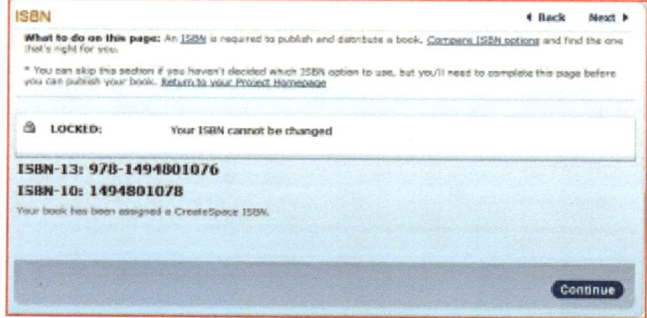

You are now the proud owner of your very own book.
Well, not so fast ...

Let's click on Continue, bottom right.

The next screen asks slightly more specific questions,
this time about our preferred Interior style and the size of
our tome. The screen will look like this:

The Interior

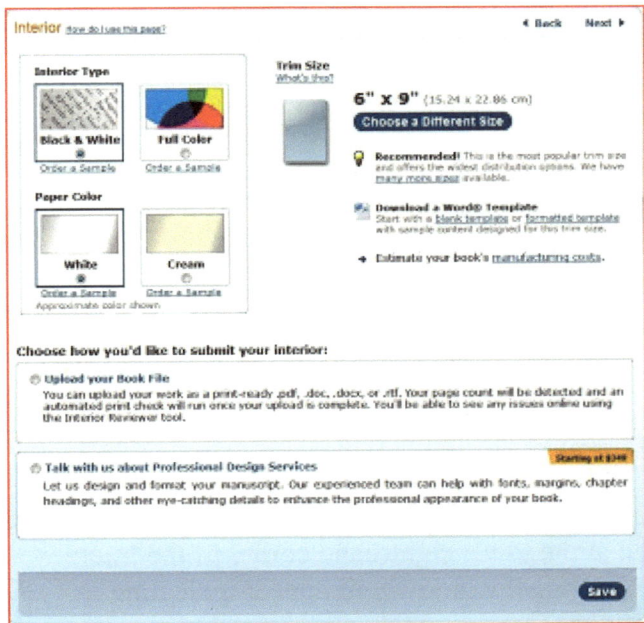

By default, the interior selected is Black & White, that I changed to Full Color, the Paper Color selected is white, and the trim size is 6" x 9". Under the trim size 6" x 9", you have a radio button that lets you choose a different size. We will not do that for our sample.

The bottom two sections on this page ask us to choose how we wish to submit the interior. This is the CONTENT of our book. We can upload our content in several formats, including print-ready, .pdf, .doc, docx, or .rtf. If we click on the first choice, "Upload your Book file," we will be shown the following half-screen that is still part of the Interior screen:

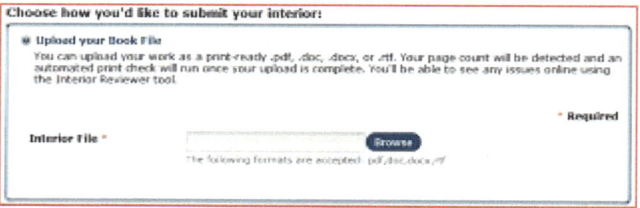

The Interior File has an address bar followed by a radio button called Browse. This is where we will upload our book contents. For our purposes, I have written and compiled this book in a file in Word that coincidentally is identical to the text herein.

Once the Word file is uploaded, I must click on the Save button at the lower right-hand corner of the Interior panel. A small window will appear indicating that my content is being uploaded, and the machinery is processing my information. Another small window will appear letting us know that the software is doing a print-check. That means that it is checking for any problems that may have occurred in the process of uploading, such as image quality, formatting issues, and the like. In our sample case, the software found 5 issues, as shown below:

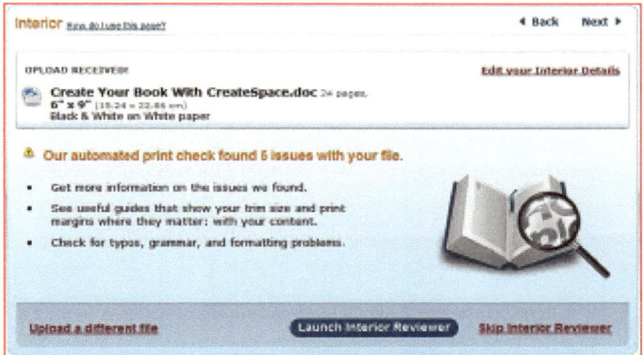

This page gives us the option of editing our interior details (top rectangle, top right-hand corner), or by uploading a different file altogether, launching the Interior Reviewer, or skipping the Interior Reviewer. For our purposes, let's click Launch Interior Reviewer. A window will appear as follows:

Interior Reviewer

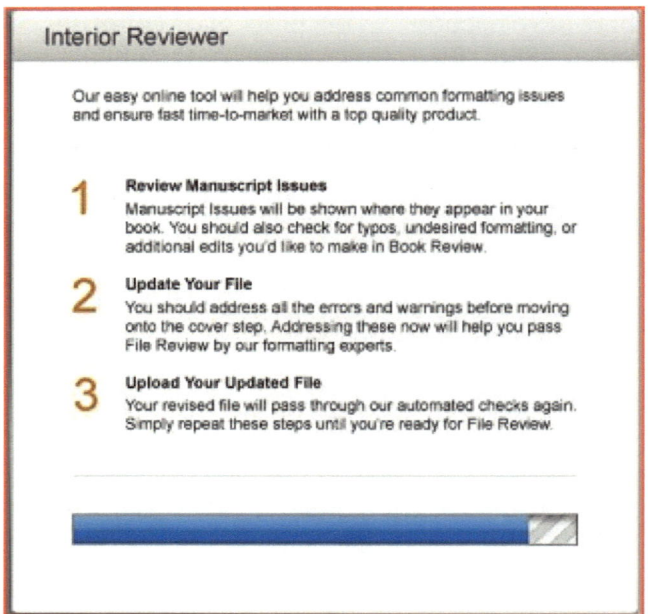

Once our book has fully uploaded, we will click on Get Started (radio button will appear at the end of the upload).

The new window will look like this:

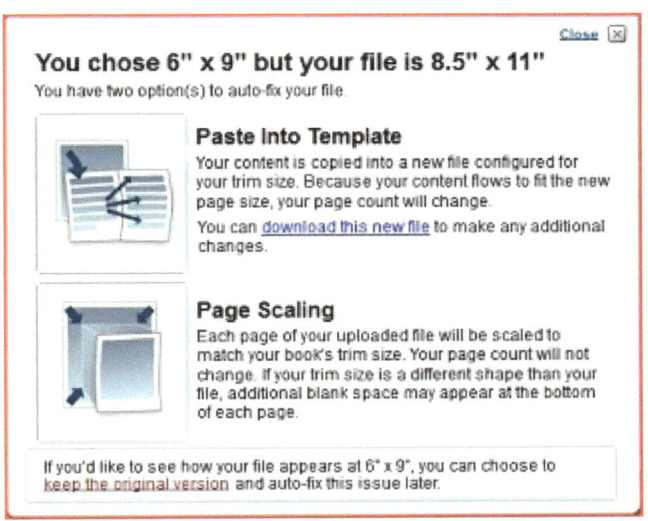

Remember that we selected the default 6" x 9" for our trim size, but the Interior Reviewer tells us that our Word file is 8.5" x 11". We will let the software do the work for us, and click on the image to the left of "Page Scaling." Once we click on Page Scaling, the Interior Reviewer will bring us to a digital version of a .pdf formatted file, with several clickable choices. The following is a partial image:

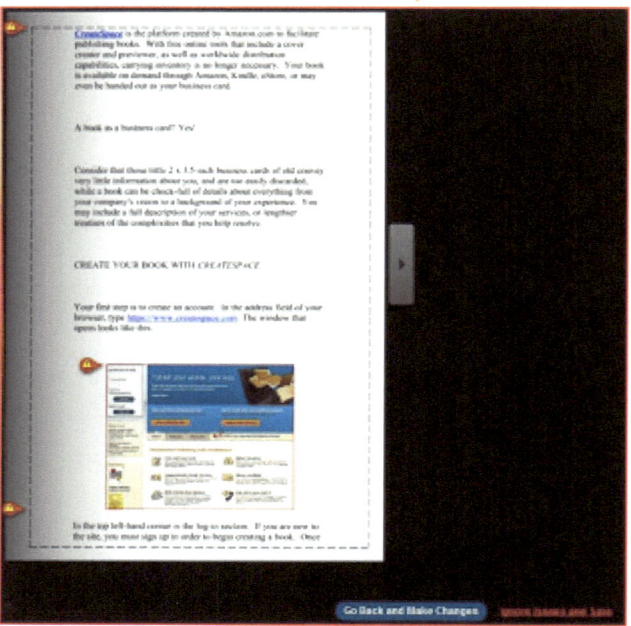

You will note that there are 3 warning icons on this page. To the right of this page (not shown) are explanations as to what those warnings refer to, including inadequate picture size, etc. Shown on the bottom right of this screen are two options, "Go Back and Make Changes," or "Ignore Issues and Save." To the left of this screen (again, not shown) is a button called "Auto-fix Trim Size" or "Download This Version (.pdf)." For our purposes, let's click on "Auto-fix Trim Size." We are once again shown the window seen earlier:

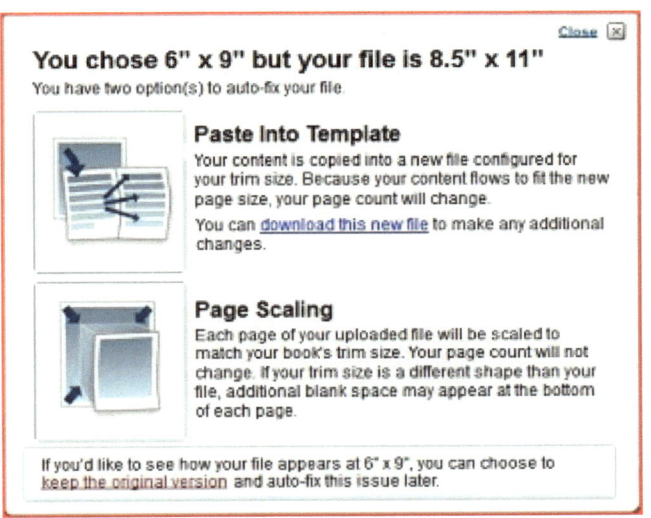

This time, we'll click on the Paste Into Template image. And presto, our fantastic, automatic Interior Reviewer has fixed all our issues, and has reorganized our Word file into a format compatible with our default trim size.

A word of advice: It would have saved us some aggravation had we anticipated these issues and written our content in Word to begin with, and by setting up our page to conform to our selected trim size of 6" x 9".

Onward ...

The cover. Once we are satisfied with the suggestions of the Interior Reviewer, we are taken to a new screen:

The Cover

We can now select from the two available options, Matte or Glossy, and by default, Glossy is selected. Below this panel are options to Build Your Cover Online, Professional Cover Design, or Upload a Print-Ready PDF Cover. Depending on your own design skills, you may select uploading your own PDF file, but for this exercise, let's choose Build Your Cover Online. Once you click on that option, the window will separate from the larger panel, and allow us to Launch Cover Creator, as follows:

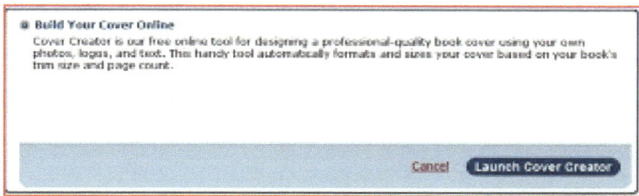

We will now click on Launch Cover Creator, bottom right.

The Cover Creator launches its front page that looks like this:

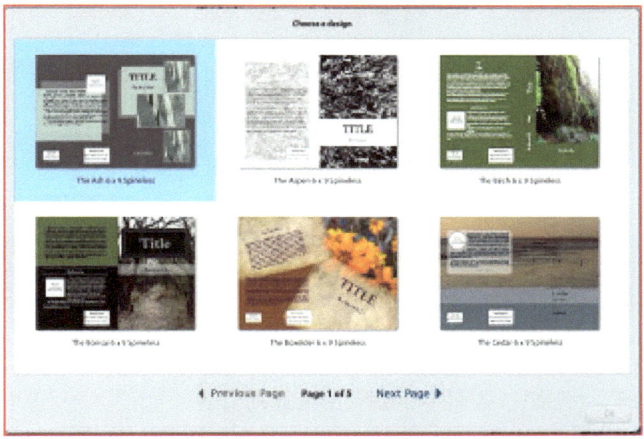

This page is only 1 of 5 similar pages, each with its own set of 6" x 9" covers, each with a different set of design and color schemes to suit just about every conceivable preference, from serious and professional to whimsical. For our purpose, I have selected the cover called The Bonsai (lower left) by clicking on the image to highlight it, then clicked OK on the bottom right corner. The following screen appears:

Task-Completion Panel

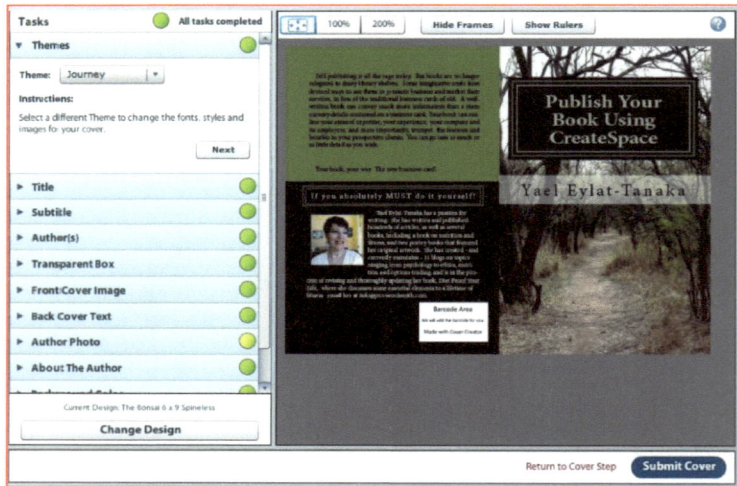

Though I love the color scheme, I think it is a little dark. Under Theme (first item in the left margin), the drop-down arrow currently indicates the theme "Journey." I will change that to "Radiance" and my Task Panel will reflect my new theme as follows:

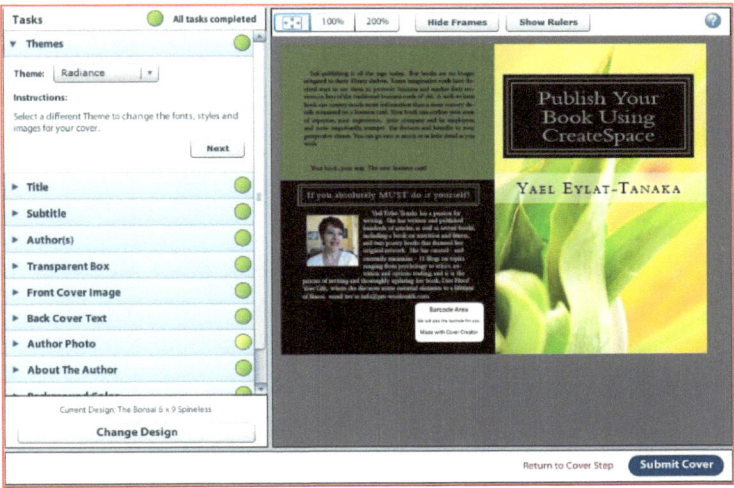

Note that the information previously entered into our Start Your New Project template (title, author, size) has automatically been inserted into my cover template. Let's go through the categories in this Task-Completion Panel.

The Tasks on the top will list how many of the 12 tasks remain to be completed. On the left are a number of entries, followed by a green button indicating their complete status. There are some items that have no circle next to them, indicating those tasks that must still be completed, such as the Background Image, for example. Let's click on that. You are then given a choice to have that section visible or not; to upload your own image or select one provided by the software. For our purposes, I'll include my own image and click upload. Once I have selected my own image, I'll click Next.

The next item to appear within the list of tasks to be completed is the back text. Again, I am asked whether I want it to be visible or not. The default is visible. Below that button is a rectangle containing gibberish. I will place my cursor within that area and begin typing my own text. Click Apply, then Next.

The following element that we are asked to complete is About The Author. Again, a space appears below that task with gibberish in Latin. I will delete that text, and enter my own. Click Apply, then Next.

The next element is selecting my Primary Background Color. The original Bonsai came with a deep, rich forest green background, but I decided to change the theme to reflect something a bit more cheerful. I was then asked to select my Secondary Background Color, and then the color of the font, each time clicking Next to get to the following element.

Even after completing all the elements to my taste, the Task list toggles back to each element from the beginning, allowing me to make changes, from the title of the book to just about every other element. I like my choices, so I will click Submit Cover on the bottom right corner.

My final cover looks like this:

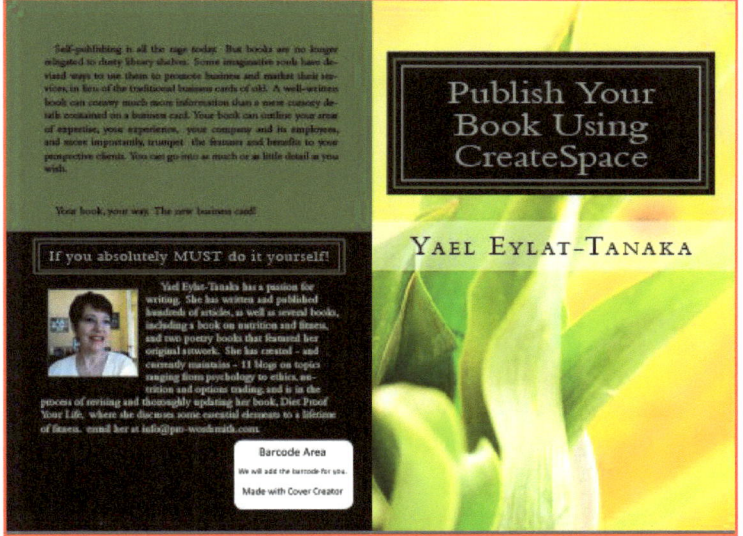

As you can see, even though I have chosen a cover template called Bonsai from the choices available through the software, I was still able to change some items as I proceeded. I was even able to change the design if I wished by clicking on the radio button at the bottom of the list called Change Design. This is what makes self-publishing fascinating and engaging.

Once we click Submit Cover on the lower right corner, we are brought once again to a screen we saw before, this time with a slight modification. It is our Build Your Cover Online screen with an option to Edit Cover (remember, we were given several options in our

previous task page), or Complete Cover. We will select
Complete Cover and click on the bottom right.

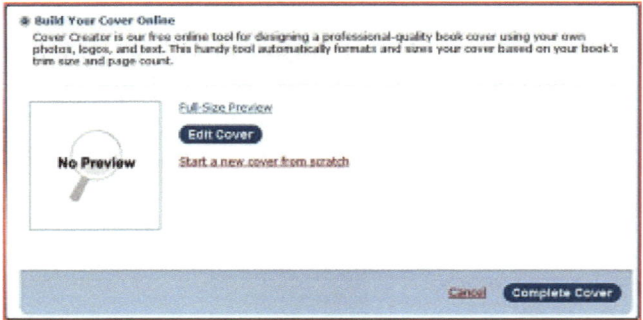

Once we click Complete Cover, we are presented with
the following screen, asking us to validate our choices:

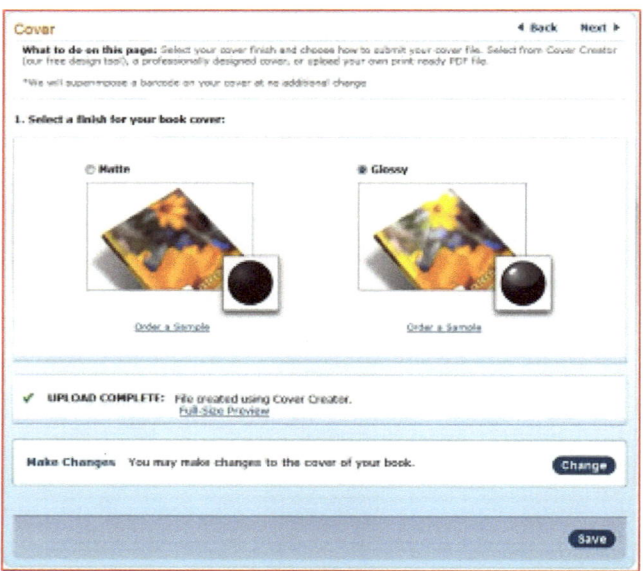

We can still change our mind about various elements if we so choose by clicking Change. But no, I think I'll stick to my choices thus far, and click Save. A confirmation page appears, where we are once again given the opportunity to change our elements (dieting should be so easy!):

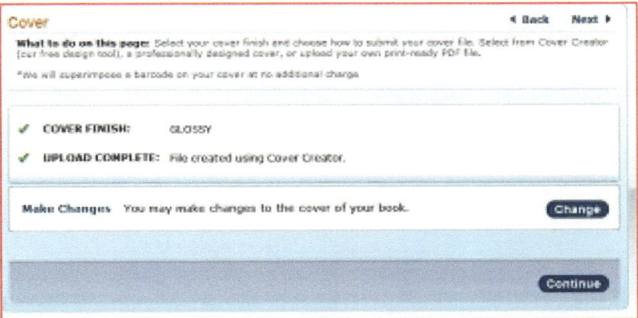

No, I don't think we should change anything, so I will click Continue.

The next page is the Complete the Setup page that confirms our previous selections, including our title with its own ISBN number, our trim size, and our choice of a glossy cover. We are getting to the tail end of our project. Let's submit our masterpiece for final review. Click the Submit Files for Review at the bottom right.

Complete the Setup

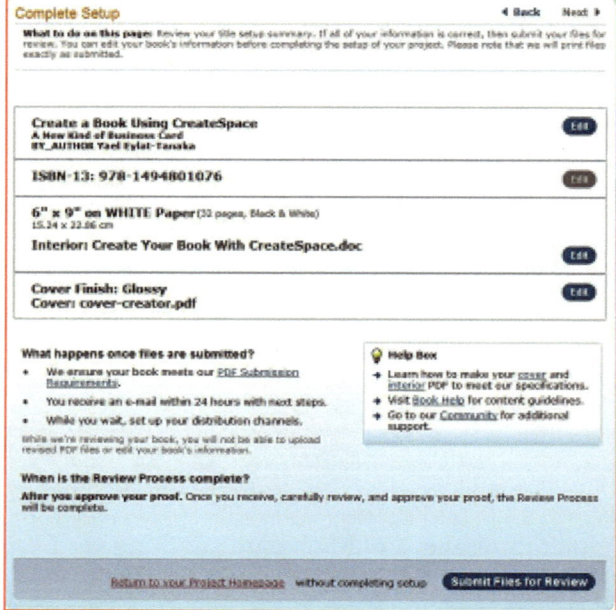

A window will tell us that Your files are being checked:

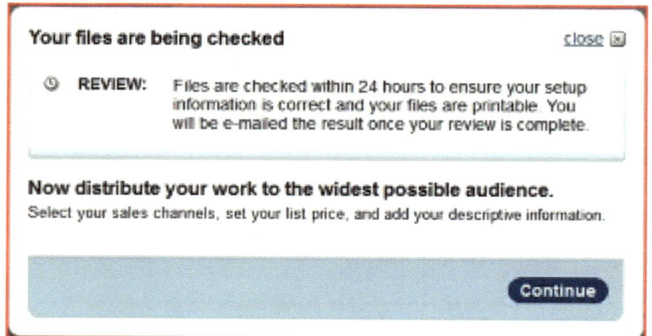

Click Continue to be taken to the Distribution Page. The Distribution part of self-publishing is really one of the most important aspects, as it makes it possible for our book to be available to the public. No longer do we need to rely on editors to promote our work, or pound the pavement drumming up business. Self-publishing now allows for every aspect of the publishing field, including the distribution of our book worldwide, and for free.

Distribution

You will note that Amazon.com and CreateSpace eStore are already selected. The bottom panel is the Expanded Distribution panel, and you may select none or all of the choices given. I selected all three. Click Save & Continue. As if the preceding wasn't enough, we now come to the really fun part: the price for our book.

Pricing

By default, we are told that the minimum price for our book must be $9.13. I put in $9.25 in the blank for USD, and clicked Save & Continue.

The next step asks us to describe the book we have written in a short paragraph, as well as select its BISAC Category (business category).

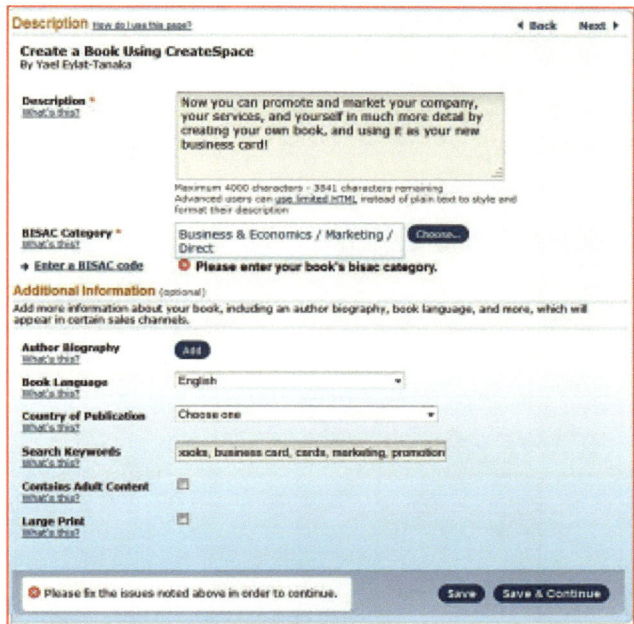

Click Save & Continue.

The reviewing process takes approximately 24 hours, after which you will be advised by email that either there are issues to be fixed, or that your files are printable, and our book meets the submission requirements.

A link (https://tsw.createspace.com/title/xxx/review) is provided within the email directing us to a panel to proof our book.

Proof Your Book

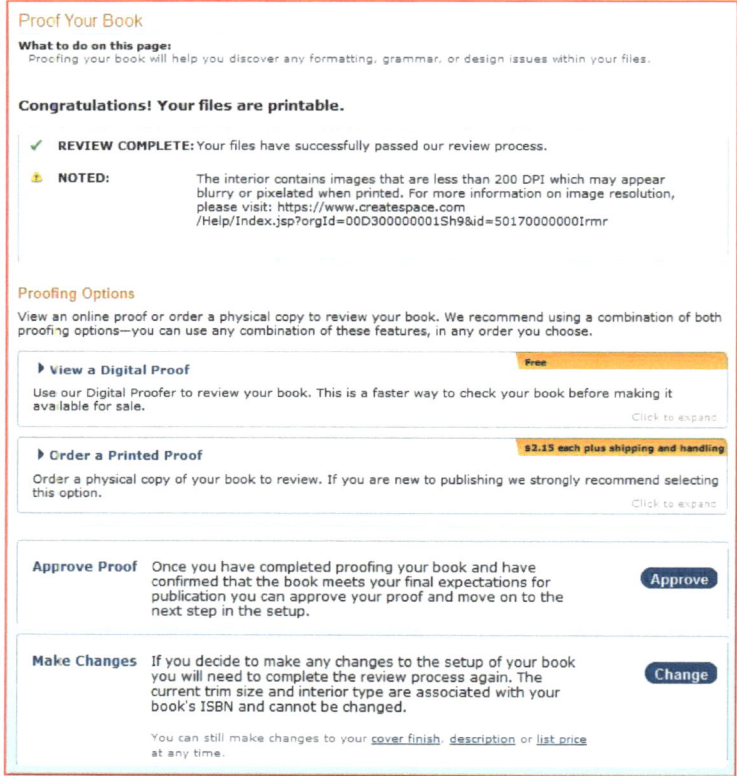

We have several options on this page. At the top, we are advised that Congratulations! Your files are printable. A bit lower on the page are our Proofing Options. These include View a Digital Proof or Order a Printed Proof. I want to see how my book will look in its current iteration, so I will click on View a Digital Proof. This will bring me to a separate screen where my book, including the cover, will be available for viewing in its final form.

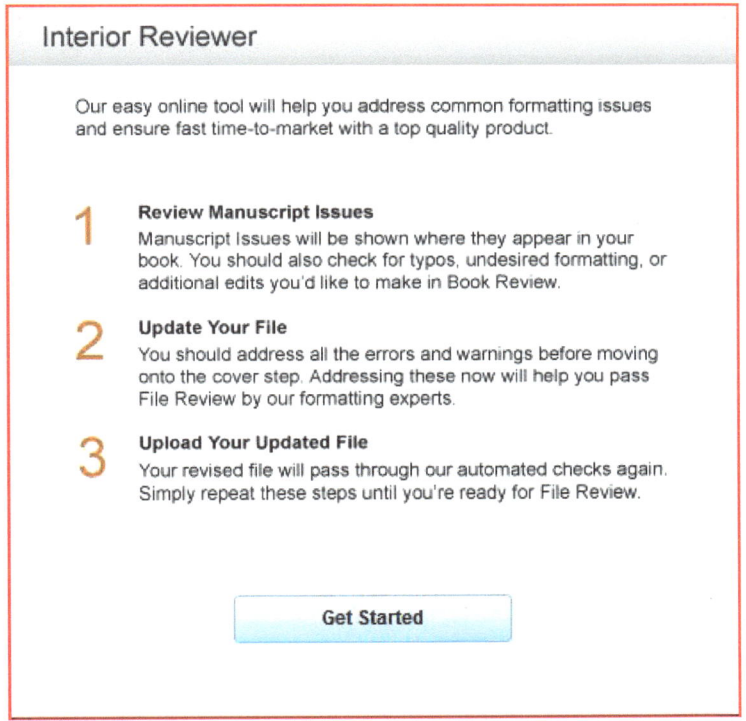

Click on Get Started on the Digital Proofer window. We can now view our finished book in digital format, toggling through the pages to review their content. The image below is a partial representation of the digital screen, with various options offered, including page numbers, Manuscript Issues, if any, listed in the right margin (not shown), the option to Go Back and Make Changes, or Save and Continue.

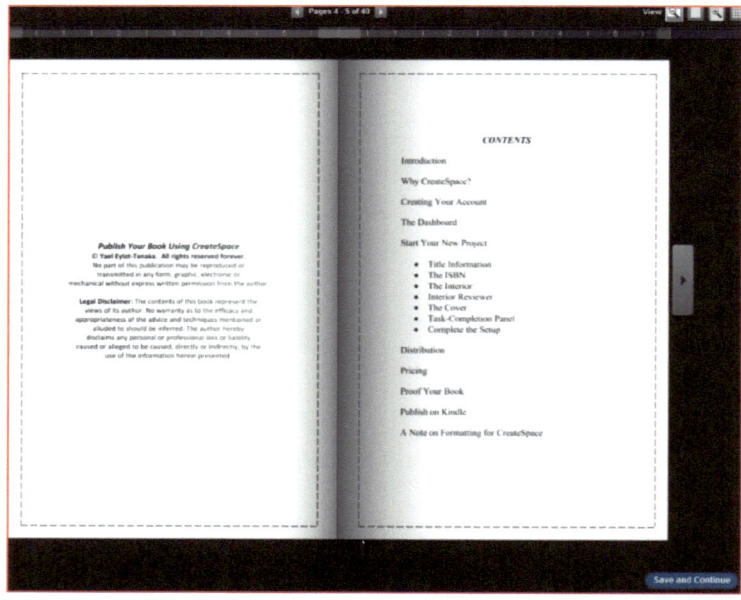

CONTENTS

I like what I see, so I will click on Save and Continue to exit the Digital Proofer to return to the Proof Your Book panel. Now I will click on Approve, and let the magic begin.

One of the last steps on the CreateSpace journey is a page that urges us to publish on Kindle. Why Kindle? Recall that both Kindle and CreateSpace are owned by Amazon.com, so there is no conflict of interest. The biggest difference between CreateSpace and Kindle, of course, is that material published on Kindle is exclusively digital, and I propose handing out your new

book in lieu of a business card, as a much more
memorable reminder.

Publish on Kindle

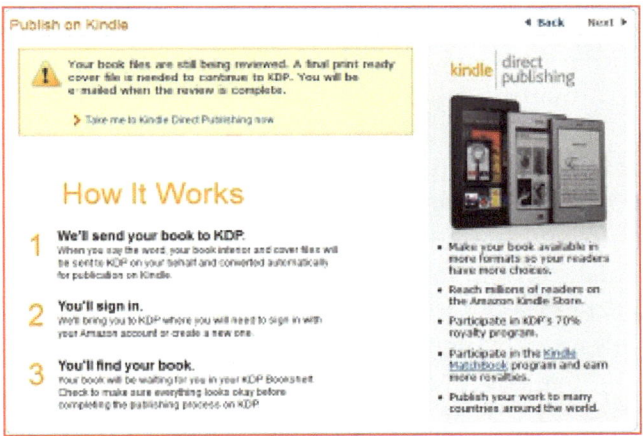

You will note from the image above that the top panel is
highlighted in yellow, indicating that my book is still
being reviewed. However, we are still able to proceed
by learning a few basics regarding publishing on Kindle.
We will therefore click on the link, "Take me to Kindle
Direct Publishing now" at the bottom of the highlighted
rectangle. But for step-by-step instructions, please see
my next book, Publish Your Book on Kindle.

A NOTE ON FORMATTING FOR CREATESPACE

In the section on Interior, above, we selected the default 6" x 9" size. Underneath that option is a section where we can download a Word template. Such template can facilitate your work, as all the formatting has already been done. For those of you who followed my instructions herein and selected the default size and formatting, you may find yourself having to do your own Word formatting.

There are many word processing programs on the market. I am not partial to any one in particular. I wrote this book almost entirely within my blog, without benefit of formatting, and then copied it into a separate Word document in order to be able to upload it into CreateSpace. Notice that all margins are set at 1".

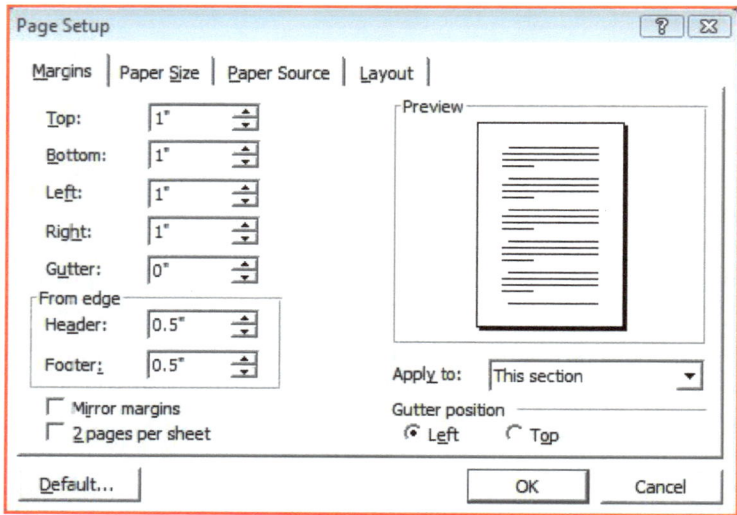

Next, click the tab for Paper Size. In order to comply as closely as possible with my selected size in CreateSpace, I chose the A5 148x210mm from the drop-down menu. Don't forget to click OK.

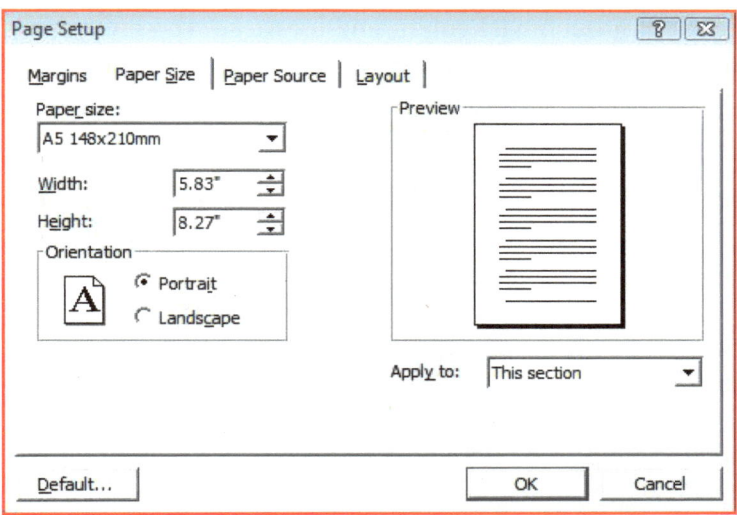

I then named my document, and uploaded it where indicated into CreateSpace (see instructions for The Interior above).

EPILOGUE

AND A SHAMELESS CALL TO ACTION

Self-publishing is a riveting and fun pursuit – for those who enjoy such challenges, and for those who have the time and patience to devote to such pursuits. If you are building a business, your efforts are no doubt better spent on details other than promoting your services. Such matters as campaigning, publicizing, or discussing benefits to your prospects is best done by you. But writing promotional letters, emails, or eNewsletters is best left to the experts.

Save yourself the aggravation, time, and money, and let me do the creative stuff behind the scenes, from ghostwriting your autobiography, to maintaining a regular blog. Contact me at info@pro-wordsmith.com NOW.

…unless you absolutely MUST do it yourself!

www.ingramcontent.com/pod-product-compliance
Lightning Source LLC
Chambersburg PA
CBHW041145180526
45159CB00002BB/735